W9-BSR-747

This book is a presentation of Weekly Reader
Books. Weekly Reader Books offers book
clubs for children from preschool through high
school. For further information write to:
WEEKLY READER BOOKS, 4343 Equity Drive,
Columbus, Ohio 43228

This edition is published by arrangement
with Rand McNally & Company.

Copyright © 1983 by Rand McNally & Company
All rights reserved
Printed in the United States of America
by Rand McNally & Company

Weekly Reader Books offers several exciting
card and activity programs. For more information,
write to WEEKLY READER BOOKS, P.O. Box 16636
Columbus, Ohio 43216.

WEEKLY READER BOOKS presents

Why Does It Rain?

A **Just Ask** Book

by Chris Arvetis

illustrated by
James Buckley

FIELD PUBLICATIONS

MIDDLETOWN, CT.

Look!
It's raining.

It's raining
all around.
Look at the big
raindrops.

Why does it rain?
I've got to find out.

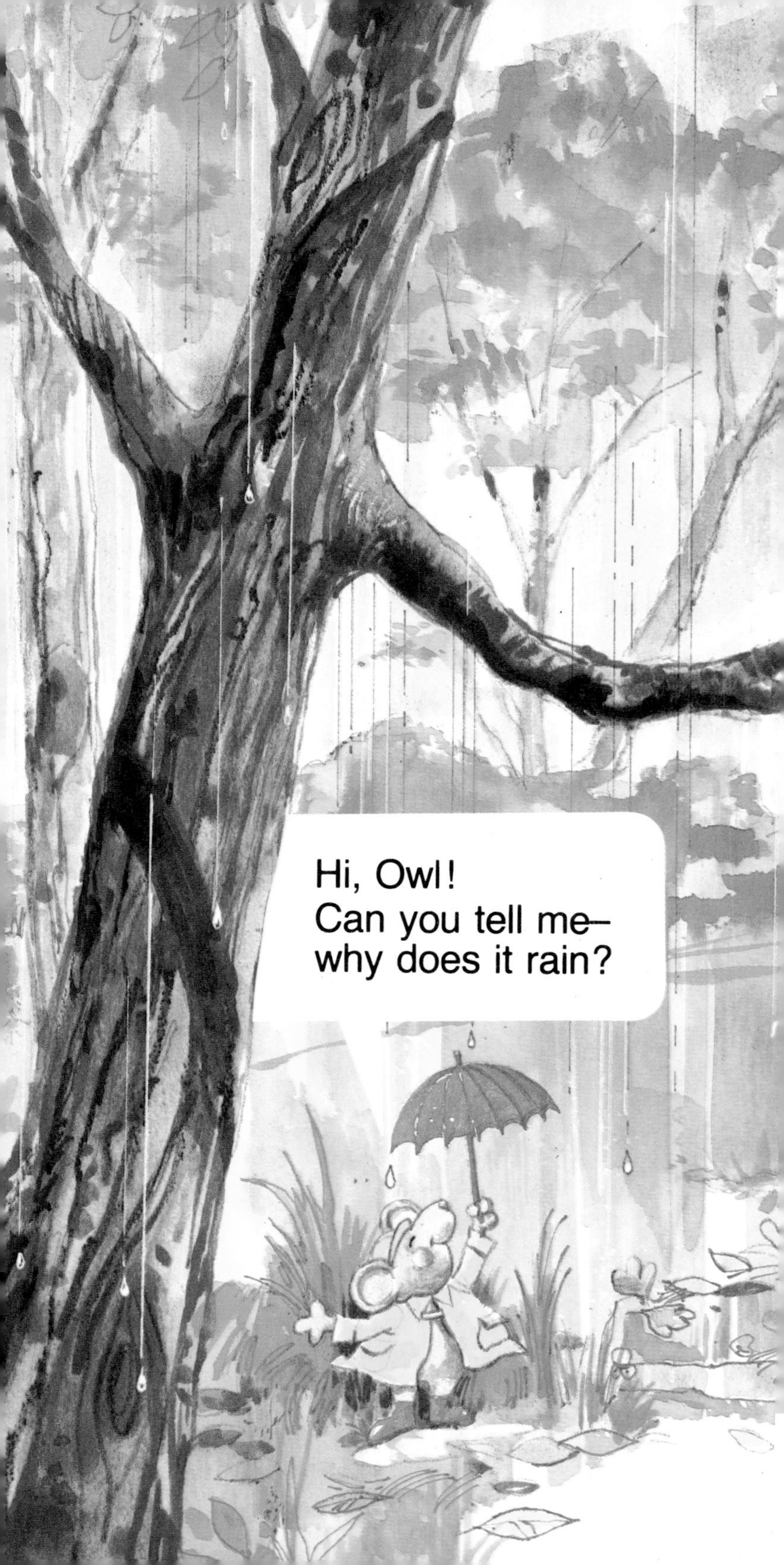
Hi, Owl! Can you tell me— why does it rain?

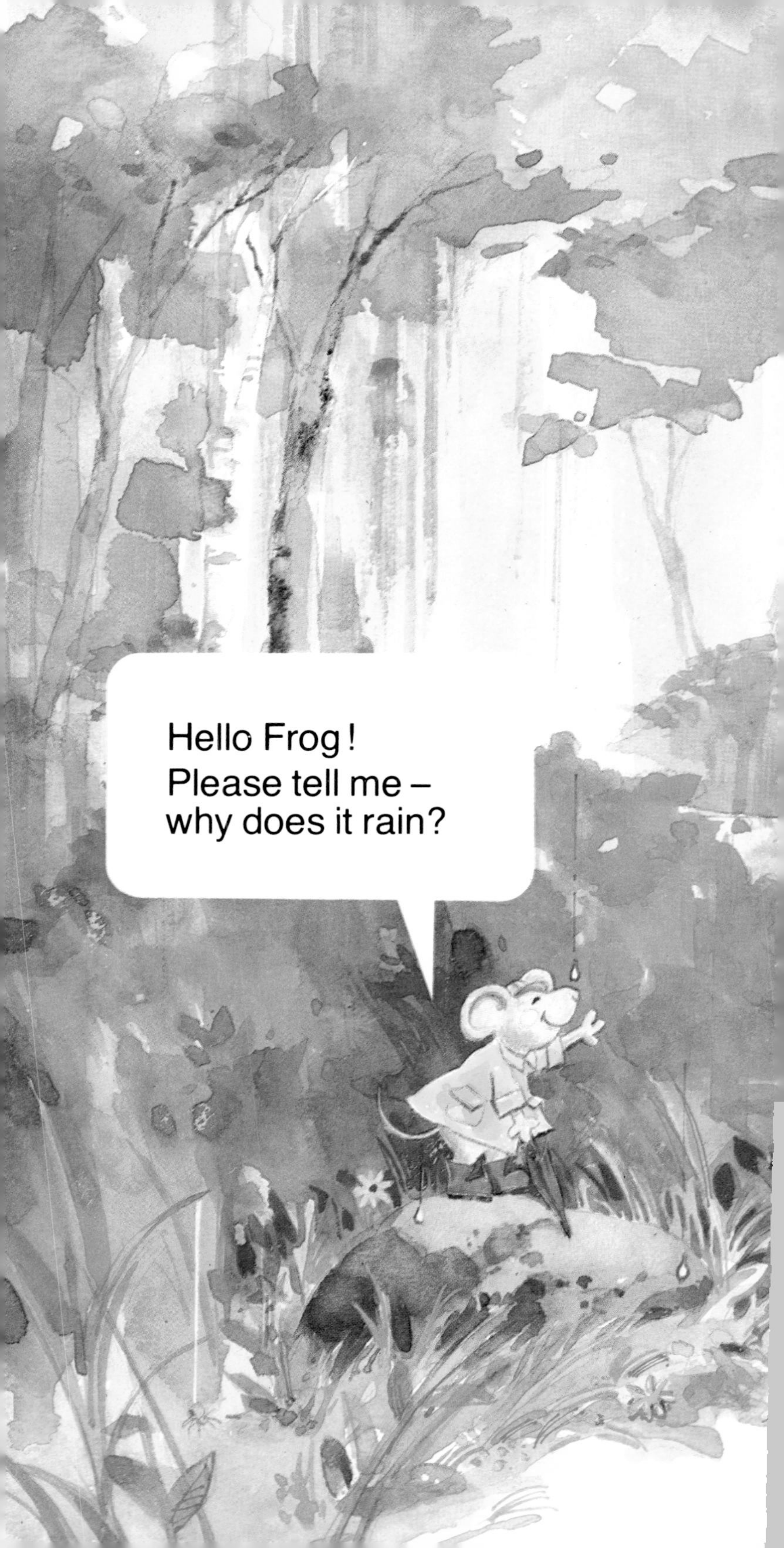
Hello Frog!
Please tell me – why does it rain?

That's a big question, but I'll tell you what I know.

Look around you.
See all the water.
See the lakes, streams,
and puddles.

When the sun shines,
it makes everything warm.
It heats the water.

As the water
is heated,
it turns into
WATER VAPOR.

You can't see
the water vapor,
but it is in the air.
It goes up
into the sky.

The puddle
is smaller!

There is a name for this.
It is a big, big word.
It's EVAPORATION.
Say it with me–
E-VAP-O-RA-TION.

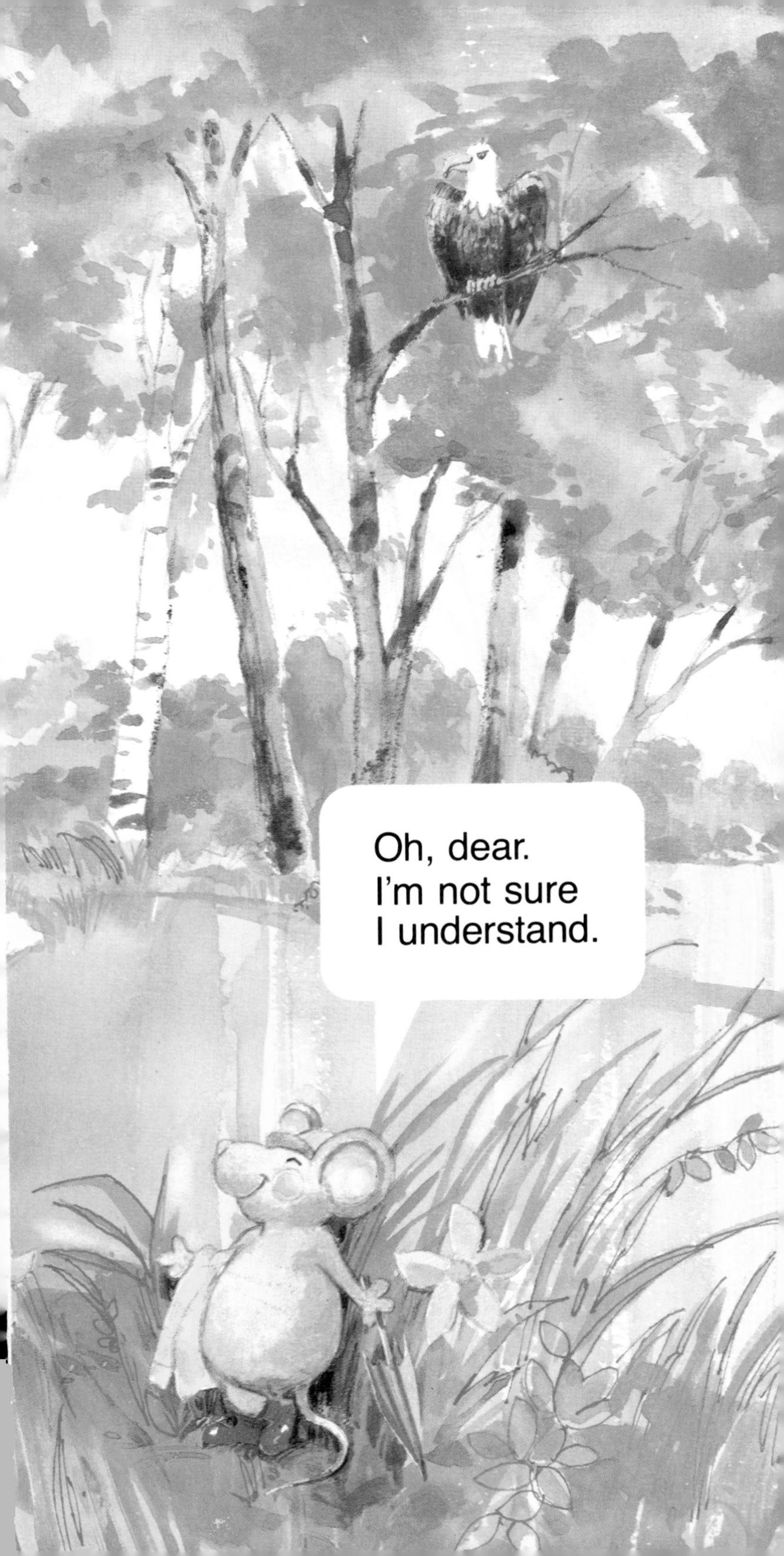
Oh, dear.
I'm not sure
I understand.

I know it's hard.
You can't see it happen.
Think of it this way:
The sun heats the water
in the puddles.
Some of the water
soaks into the ground.
Some of the water
evaporates, or goes
up into the air.

I'll take him for a ride.

When it goes up into the air– that's EVAPORATION.
Okay! But then what happens?

Let me tell you. I'll take you into the sky to show you what happens next.

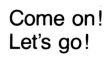

As we go up, the air gets cooler and cooler.

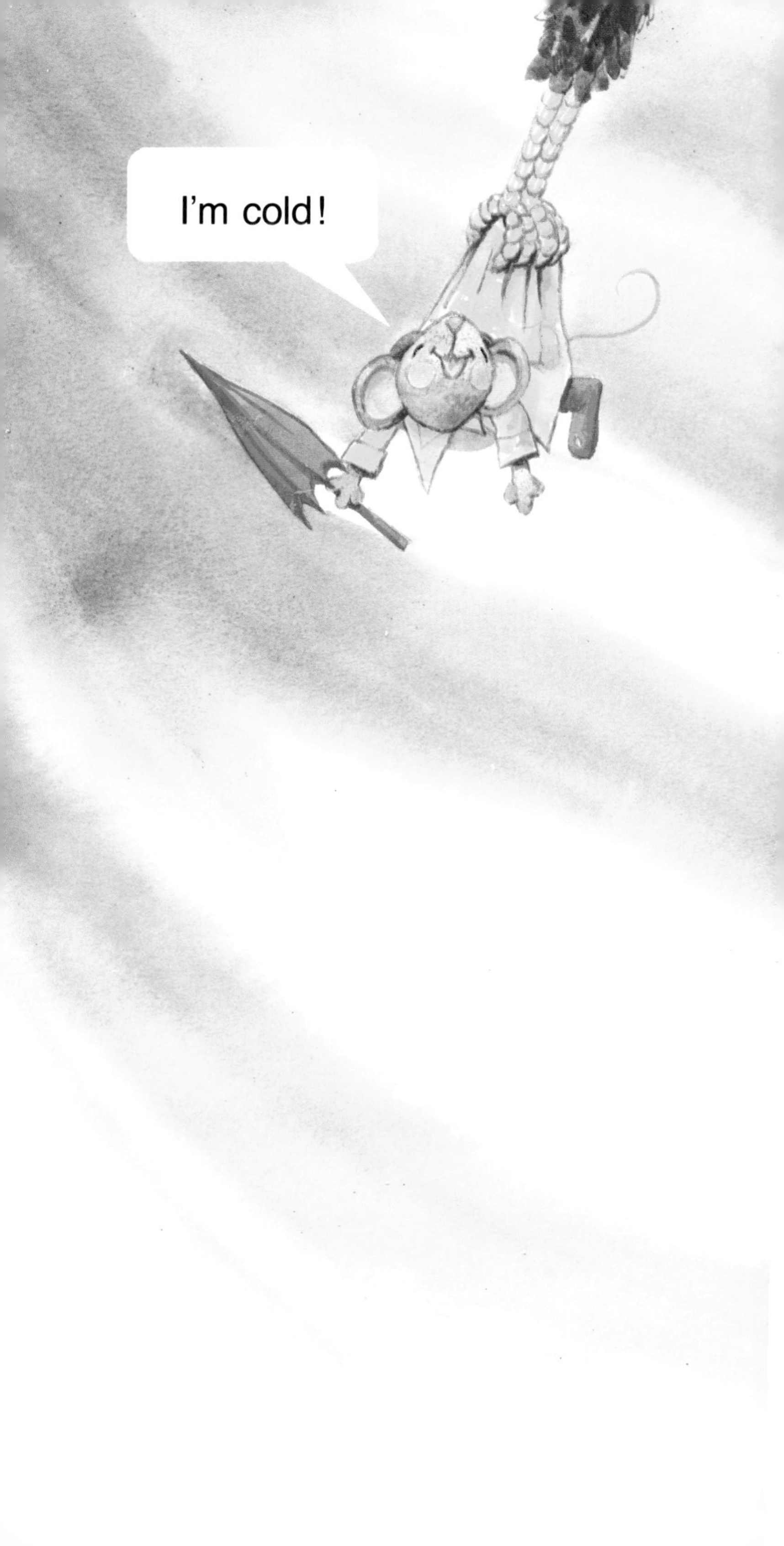
I'm cold!

That's what
happens to the
water vapor.
As it goes up,
it gets cooler
and cooler.

Looks like
rain!

No doubt!

As the water vapor cools, it forms teeny, tiny drops of water.

When there are
a lot of these
tiny drops of water,
a cloud is formed.

As the air cools more, the tiny drops in the cloud stick together.

The drops get
bigger and heavier.
When they get too big
and heavy, they fall
to the ground.
Hey, wait for me!

Let's
get out
of here!

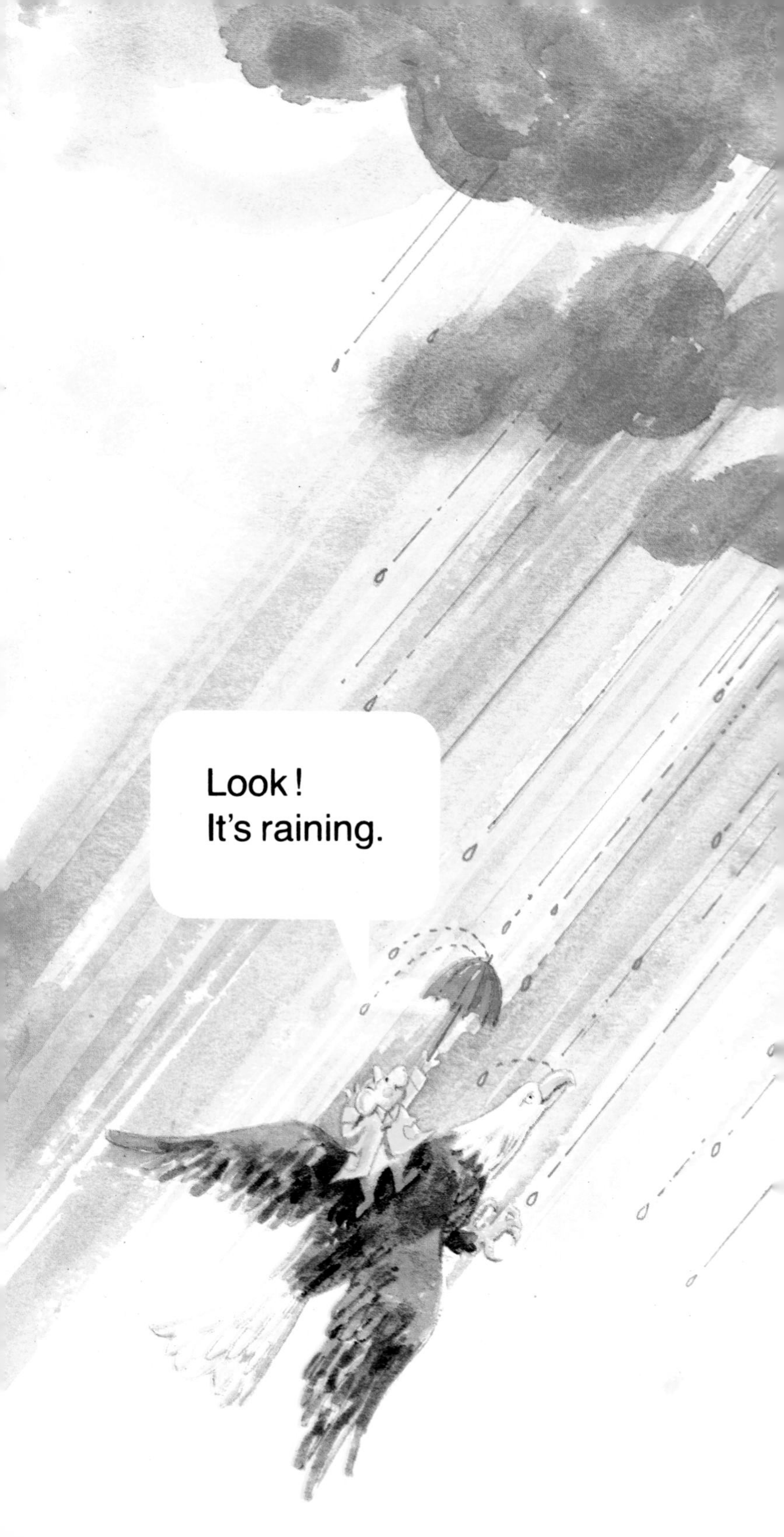
Look! It's raining.